ITALIAN RECIPES

"Cook like a real Italian mother"

In this book, all the recipes that Italian mothers cook every day for their families have been collected. Of course the variations are innumerable but the basic ingredients are the original ones.

RECIPE INDEX:

Spaghetti Carbonara

INGREDIENTS

100g pancetta
50g pecorino cheese
50g parmesan
3 large eggs
350g spaghetti
2 plump garlic cloves, peeled and left whole
50g unsalted butter

sea salt and freshly ground black pepper.

Method

STEP 1
Put a large saucepan of water on to boil.

STEP 2
Finely chop the 100g pancetta, having first removed any rind. Finely grate 50g pecorino cheese and 50g parmesan and mix them together.

STEP 3
Beat the 3 large eggs in a medium bowl and season with a little freshly grated black pepper. Set everything aside.

STEP 4
Add 1 tsp salt to the boiling water, add 350g spaghetti and when the water comes back to the boil, cook at a constant simmer, covered, for 10 minutes or until al dente (just cooked).

STEP 5
Squash 2 peeled plump garlic cloves with the blade of a knife, just to bruise it.

STEP 6
While the spaghetti is cooking, fry the pancetta with the garlic. Drop 50g unsalted butter into a large frying pan or wok and, as soon as the butter has melted, tip in the pancetta and garlic.

STEP 7
Leave to cook on a medium heat for about 5 minutes, stirring often, until the pancetta is golden and crisp. The garlic has now imparted its flavour, so take it out with a slotted spoon and discard.

STEP 8
Keep the heat under the pancetta on low. When the pasta is ready, lift it from the water with a pasta fork or tongs and put it in the frying pan with the pancetta. Don't worry if a little water drops in the pan as well (you want this to happen) and don't throw the pasta water away yet.

STEP 9
Mix most of the cheese in with the eggs, keeping a small handful back for sprinkling over later.

STEP 10
Take the pan of spaghetti and pancetta off the heat. Now quickly pour in the eggs and cheese. Using the tongs or a long fork, lift up the spaghetti so it mixes easily with the egg mixture, which thickens but doesn't scramble, and everything is coated.

STEP 11
Add extra pasta cooking water to keep it saucy (several tablespoons should do it). You don't want it wet, just moist. Season with a little salt, if needed.

STEP 12
Use a long-pronged fork to twist the pasta on to the serving plate or bowl. Serve immediately with a little sprinkling of the remaining cheese and a grating of black pepper. If the dish does get a little dry before serving,

splash in some more hot pasta water
and the glossy sauciness will be revived.

Lasagna Bolognese

INGREDIENTS

FOR THE BOLOGNESE
2 tbsp. extra-virgin olive oil
1 large onion, chopped
1 large carrot, peeled and finely chopped
2 stalks celery, finely chopped
3 cloves garlic, minced
2 lb. ground beef
1/2 c. dry white wine
2 (28-oz.) cans crushed tomatoes
1/4 c. tomato paste
1 c. low-sodium beef (or chicken) broth
1 bay leaf

1 c. whole milk
Kosher salt
Freshly ground black pepper

FOR THE LASAGNA
1 lb. lasagna noodles
3 c. ricotta
1 large egg, beaten
1 c. freshly grated Parmesan, divided
1 1/2 tsp. dried oregano
1/4 tsp. crushed red pepper flakes
Kosher salt
Freshly ground black pepper
1 lb. fresh mozzarella, sliced
Freshly chopped parsley, for serving

Method

STEP 1
In a large dutch oven over
medium-high heat, heat oil. Add onion,
carrot, and celery, and cook until soft, 5
minutes. Add garlic and cook until
fragrant, 1 minute more. Stir in beef
breaking up meat with back of a spoon.
Cook until no longer pink, about 8
minutes.

STEP 2
Add wine, and bring mixture to a simmer. Cook until wine is mostly reduced. Stir in tomatoes, tomato paste, stock, and bay leaf, then reduce heat and simmer for 1 hour, allowing flavors to meld.

STEP 3
Discard bay leaf, then gradually stir in milk. Let simmer, stirring occasionally, until milk is fully incorporated, about 45 minutes. Season with salt and pepper.

STEP 4
Assemble lasagna: Preheat oven to 375°. In a large pot of boiling salted water, cook pasta according to package directions. Drain.

STEP 5
In a medium bowl, combine ricotta, egg, ¾ cup Parmesan, oregano, and red pepper flakes. Season with salt and pepper.

STEP 6

Add a thin layer of bolognese to the bottom of a 9"-x-13" baking dish. Add a layer of noodles then top with ricotta mixture and sauce, then repeat layers. Top last layer of noodles with bolognese, mozzarella, and remaining ¼ cup Parmesan.

STEP 7

Cover with foil and bake for 40 minutes, then remove foil and bake 20 minutes or until cheese is melty and sauce is bubbling.

STEP 8

Garnish with parsley before serving.

Pasta Puttanesca

INGREDIENTS

1/4 c. extra-virgin olive oil
4 cloves garlic, smashed
4 anchovy fillets, chopped
1 (28-oz.) diced tomatoes
1/2 c. kalamata olives, pitted
1/4 c. capers
1/2 tsp. crushed red pepper flakes
Kosher salt
1 lb. spaghetti
Chopped parsley, for garnish

Freshly grated Parmesan, for serving

Method

STEP 1
In a large skillet or pot over medium
heat, heat oil. Add garlic and cook until
fragrant, 1 minute. Add anchovies and
cook until fragrant, another minute.
Add tomatoes, olives, capers, and red
pepper flakes. Bring to a boil, then
reduce heat and let simmer, 15 minutes.

STEP 2
Meanwhile, bring a large pot of salted
water to a boil. Add spaghetti and cook
according to package directions, until al
dente; drain. Toss spaghetti in sauce.
Sprinkle with parsley and Parmesan
and serve.

Italian Pasta Salad

INGREDIENTS

FOR THE PASTA
16 oz. fusilli pasta, cooked according to
package instructions
8 oz. mozzarella balls, halved
4 oz. salami, quartered
2 c. baby spinach
1 c. cherry tomatoes, halved
1 c. artichoke hearts, chopped
1/2 c. pitted black olives, sliced

FOR THE DRESSING
1/3 c. extra-virgin olive oil
2 tbsp. red wine vinegar
1 garlic clove, minced
2 tsp. Italian seasoning
1 tbsp. freshly chopped parsley
Pinch red pepper flakes
Kosher salt
Freshly ground black pepper

Method

STEP 1
In a large bowl, toss together pasta, mozzarella, salami, spinach, tomatoes, artichokes, and olives.

STEP 2
To make the dressing, add olive oil, vinegar, garlic, Italian seasoning, parsley, and red pepper flakes to a jar and secure with a lid then shake to combine. Season with salt and pepper to taste.

STEP 3
Dress pasta with dressing and serve.

Pasta and Beans

INGREDIENTS

1 cup ditalini or 1 cup elbow macaroni, uncooked
1 tablespoon olive oil or 1 tablespoon vegetable oil
1 medium onion, finely chopped
1 carrot, finely chopped
1 stalk celery, finely chopped
1 clove garlic, minced
1 can cannellini beans, drained and rinsed (white kidney beans)
1(14 1/2 ounce) can diced tomatoes
1/2 teaspoon salt
1/4 teaspoon black pepper

4 cups water
1⁄4 cup grated parmesan cheese or 1/4 cup locatelli cheese
1⁄4 cup chopped fresh parsley

Method
Cook pasta as the box instructs, in boiling salted water.
While pasta is cooking, heat oil in a large saucepan over medium heat until hot.
Add onion, carrot and celery and cook for 15 minutes or until tender, stirring occasionally.
Add garlic and cook one minute more.
Add beans, tomatoes, salt, pepper, and water and heat to boiling over high heat.
Reduce heat to low-med heat and simmer, uncovered for 20 minutes.
Stir in drained pasta, cheese and parsley and cook until heated through.

Seafood Spaghetti

INGREDIENTS

¼ cup extra-virgin olive oil
1 medium onion, finely chopped
4 garlic cloves, sliced
¾ teaspoon crushed red pepper flakes
3 tablespoons tomato paste
1 cup dry white wine
1 28-ounce can whole peeled tomatoes
Kosher salt
1 pound spaghetti
2 pounds mussels, scrubbed, debearded

2 pounds large shrimp, peeled,
deveined
3 tablespoons unsalted butter
3 tablespoons finely chopped parsley
1 tablespoon fresh lemon juice
Lemon wedges (for serving)

Method

STEP 1
Heat oil in a large heavy pot over
medium. Cook onion, stirring
occasionally, until golden and softened,
8–10 minutes. Add garlic and red
pepper flakes and season with salt.
Cook, stirring often, until fragrant and
garlic is softened, about 2 minutes. Add
tomato paste and cook, stirring
occasionally, until slightly darkened in
color and starts sticking to bottom of
pan, about 4 minutes. Add wine and
cook, stirring often, until the smell of
the alcohol is almost completely gone,
about 4 minutes. Add tomatoes and
juices, crushing with your hands, and
increase heat to medium-high. Cook,
stirring often, until sauce thickens
slightly, 8–10 minutes. Taste and
season sauce with salt.

STEP 2

Meanwhile, cook pasta in a large pot of boiling salted water, stirring occasionally, until very al dente, about 3 minutes less than package directions. Drain, reserving 1 cup pasta cooking liquid.

STEP 3

Add mussels, shrimp, and ¼ cup pasta cooking liquid to sauce. Cover and cook, shaking pot occasionally, until mussels open, about 4 minutes. Using tongs, pick out shrimp and mussels and transfer to a large bowl, discarding any mussels that have not opened. Loosely cover with foil to keep warm.

STEP 4

Add pasta and another ¼ cup pasta cooking liquid to sauce and stir to coat. Reduce heat to medium, add butter, and continue to cook, stirring and adding more pasta cooking liquid as needed, until sauce coats pasta, about 4 minutes. Remove from heat, return shrimp and mussels to pot, and

carefully toss to combine. Mix in
parsley and lemon juice.

STEP 5
Transfer pasta to a platter and serve
with lemon wedges for squeezing over.

Cannelloni

INGREDIENTS

SAUCE:
1 tbsp olive oil
1 garlic clove , finely chopped
1 small onion , finely chopped
800 g / 28 oz crushed tomato
1 cup water (swirl in tomato can to clean out)
3/4 tsp salt + pepper to taste
Handful basil leaves , torn, or 1 tsp dried herbs (e.g. Italian mix, oregano, thyme, basil)

FILLING:

250 g / 8 oz frozen chopped spinach , thawed (Note 1)
500 g / 1 lb ricotta , full fat please (Note 2)
1/3 cup grated parmesan
1 cup shredded cheese (Mozzarella, Colby, Cheddar, Tasty, Gruyere, Swiss)
1 egg
1 large garlic clove , minced
Grated fresh nutmeg (just a sprinkling) or 1/8 tsp nutmeg powder (optional)
1/2 tsp salt and pepper , each

CANNELLONI
18 - 22 dried cannelloni tubes (Note 3)
1 - 1 1/2 cups shredded Mozzarella
More basil , for garnish (optional)

Method

SAUCE:
Heat oil in a large skillet over medium high heat. Add garlic and onion, cook for 2 - 3 minutes until translucent. Add tomato, water, salt and pepper.
Stir, reduce heat to medium, simmer for 5 minutes. Optional: add 1/2 cup water and blend sauce until smooth (I do this for guests!).

Stir through basil or dried herbs. Set aside.

FILLING:
Place spinach in a colander and press out most of the liquid (don't need to thoroughly squeeze dry).
Place Spinach in bowl with remaining Filling ingredients. Mix, taste, adjust salt and pepper to taste (different cheeses have different saltiness).

ASSEMBLE & BAKE:
Preheat the oven to 180C/350F.
Choose a baking pan which will comfortably fit about 20 cannelloni - mine is 21 x 26 cm / 8.5 x 10.5".
Spread a bit of Sauce on the base.
Transfer Filling to a piping bag with a large nozzle (that fits in the tubes), or use a strong ziplock bag. Or do this step using a knife (it's a bit tedious though!).
Pipe the filling into the tubes. Place in baking dish.
Pour over remaining Sauce, covering all the tubes. Cover with foil, then bake for 25 minutes.

Remove foil, scatter over cheese.
Return to oven for 10 minutes until
cheese is melted.
Serve, garnished with extra basil if
desired.

Recipe Notes:

1. Spinach - I use frozen spinach for the
convenience and also because I'm a
sucker for the whole "snap frozen"
thing. To use fresh, use about 500g/1 lb
sliced spinach leaves or baby spinach
leaves, saute with a little oil to wilt
down and remove excess liquid. Cool
then proceed with recipe.

2. Ricotta - Low fat ricotta is harder and
drier, so it's more difficult to pipe into
the tubes plus once baked, is not as
juicy and moist. Avoid Perfect Italian
brand in tubs. My favourite is
Paesanella.

3. Cannelloni - The cannelloni tubes I
use are the dried ones sold in boxes at
supermarkets and delis. They are about
11 cm / 4" long and 2.5cm / 1" wide.

They do not need to be boiled before cooking in the oven.

This recipe can also be used for manicotti which are larger tubes with ridges - use 10 to 12.

You can also make this using fresh lasagna sheets. Just roll Filling up inside, place in the baking pan seam side down. I prefer using dried tubes - refer in post for the reason why.

4. For FREEZING or refrigerating uncooked: Add extra 3/4 cup water* into Sauce, cook Sauce per recipe then blend* until smooth. Place filled, uncooked cannelloni in single or multiple dishes, cover with sauce then cheese. Cover, cool then freeze / refrigerate.

On the day of, thaw then bake per recipe (covered then uncovered). OR bake from frozen, bake covered 35 minutes then uncovered 10 minutes.

* The reason for extra water and blending: When uncooked cannelloni is assembled, the dry pasta will absorb some of the liquid as it freezes. If you don't add extra water, the sauce dries up once baked. Blending also helps

here, plus it brings the sauce together better so it doesn't split when thawed. COOKED leftovers - refrigerate up to 3 days or freeze, thaw, then reheat covered in microwave for best results.

5. Nutrition per serving, assuming 5 servings.

Pasta al Pesto

INGREDIENTS

2 cups fresh basil leaves, packed (can
sub half the basil leaves with baby
spinach)
1/2 cup freshly grated Romano or
Parmesan-Reggiano cheese (about 2
ounces)
1/2 cup extra virgin olive oil
1/3 cup pine nuts (can sub chopped
walnuts)

3 garlic cloves, minced (about 3
teaspoons)
1/4 teaspoon salt, more to taste
1/8 teaspoon freshly ground black
pepper, more to taste

Method

STEP 1
Pulse basil and pine nuts in a food
processor
Place the basil leaves and pine nuts into
the bowl of a food processor and pulse a
several times.

STEP 2
Add the garlic and cheese
Add the garlic and Parmesan or
Romano cheese and pulse several times
more. Scrape down the sides of the food
processor with a rubber spatula.

STEP 3
Stream in the olive oil
While the food processor is running,
slowly add the olive oil in a steady small
stream. Adding the olive oil slowly,
while the processor is running, will help
it emulsify and help keep the olive oil

from separating. Occasionally stop to scrape down the sides of the food processor.

STEP 4
Stir in salt and freshly ground black pepper, add more to taste
Toss with pasta for a quick sauce, dollop over baked potatoes, or spread onto crackers or toasted slices of bread.

Pasta all' Arrabbiata

INGREDIENTS

3 tablespoons kosher salt
4 tablespoons extra-virgin olive oil, plus
4 more tablespoons
½ cup tomato paste
1 tablespoon hot red-pepper flakes
1 ½ cups chopped tomatoes, like Pomì
1 pound penne
Maldon or other flaky sea salt
Freshly grated Parmigiano-Reggiano
for serving.

Method

STEP 1
Bring 6 quarts of water to a boil in a large pot, and add 3 tablespoons of kosher salt.

STEP 2
Meanwhile, put 4 tablespoons of olive oil in a large sauté pan over medium heat, and then add the tomato paste and pepper flakes; reduce the heat to low and stir just until fragrant, about 4 minutes. Stir in the tomatoes, and remove from the heat.
STEP 3
Drop the pasta into the boiling water, and cook until al dente. Drain the pasta, reserving 1/4 cup of the pasta water.

STEP 4
Add the pasta and the reserved pasta water to the tomato sauce, stir and toss over medium heat until the pasta is well coated. Season with salt if necessary, then add the remaining oil, tossing well. Serve immediately, with grated Parmigiano-Reggiano on the side.

Gnocchi alla Sorrentina

INGREDIENTS

GNOCCHI ALLA SORRENTINA
600g of floury potatoes
150g of plain flour
2 egg yolks
250g of mozzarella cheese, torn into
small chunks
8 basil leaves, roughly torn
pecorino, grated

sea salt

TO MAKE THE TOMATO SAUCE
600g of passata
4 tbsp of extra virgin olive oil
2 garlic cloves, peeled and crushed
salt
pepper.

Method

STEP1
Boil the potatoes whole, skin on, until cooked through. Drain then transfer to a frying pan set over a low heat. Gently heat the potatoes until they feel dry on all sides. Allow them to cool

STEP 2
To make the tomato sauce, place the oil and the garlic in a medium saucepan set over a medium heat. Add the passata and 60ml water, cover and allow the sauce to cook for 30 minutes, stirring often. Taste, season and keep warm

STEP 3

Peel the skins from the cooled potatoes
and discard

STEP 4
Scatter three-quarters of the flour over
a work surface. Press the potato though
a ricer onto the flour, form the mixture
into a well and add the egg yolks. Shape
everything into a soft dough, gradually
adding the flour until you form a soft
pliable texture. Dust the work surface
with a little more flour and divide the
dough into 4

STEP 5
Roll out the dough into long cylinders,
about the thickness of your thumb. Cut
each length into segments, then press
each one onto a gnocchi board or fork
to give them a ridged texture. Reserve
on a flour-lined tray

STEP 6
Preheat the oven to 200°C/gas mark 5

STEP 7
Bring a large pot of heavily salted water
to a rolling boil. Add the gnocchi and
cook until they float on the surface, this

should take approximately 3 minutes.
Drain with a slotted spoon and place in
the tomato sauce

STEP 8
Stir and transfer to an oven-proof dish.
Dress with the mozzarella and basil,
dust with grated pecorino and cover
with foil. Bake for 10 minutes, until the
mozzarella has melted. Remove the foil
and finish under the grill for 2–3
minutes, until the cheese is golden.
Serve immediately.

Supplì al Telefono

INGREDIENTS

1 small onion, diced
1 garlic clove, sliced
150g of beef mince
2 sprigs of thyme, leaves picked
100ml of red wine
400g of passata
200g of risotto rice
200ml of beef stock
1 knob of butter
10g of Parmesan, grated

125g of buffalo mozzarella
1 egg
50g of flour
100g of breadcrumbs
olive oil

Method

STEP 1
To begin, sauté the onions and garlic in a glug of olive oil until soft. Add the mince and thyme leaves and cook until the mince is nicely browned

STEP 2
Add the red wine and reduce by half. Next, add the passata and leave to simmer for 20 minutes

STEP 3
Add the risotto rice and cook until it has absorbed most of the passata. After this time, add a couple of splashes of beef stock and again wait for the rice to absorb the liquid. Repeat the process, adding a small amount at a time, until the rice is almost ready but a little undercooked. Remove from the heat

STEP 4
Stir in the butter and grated Parmesan, then spread over a cling film-lined tray to allow the rice to cool quickly. Chill in the fridge overnight or until completely cold and set

STEP 5
Tear the mozzarella into 12 even strips and, using a knife, cut the set rice into 12 even portions

STEP 6
Take one of the portions of rice, lay it flat in your hand, and place the mozzarella in the centre. Roll the rice and around until you have a nice neat cylinder. Place on a clean plate and repeat to form the remaining supplì

STEP 7
Preheat a deep-fryer or deep pan of oil to 180°C

STEP 8
Prepare a bowl of whisked egg, a plate of flour and a tray of breadcrumbs. One-by-one, roll the supplì in the flour,

then the egg, and finally coat in the breadcrumbs

STEP 9
Deep-fry the supplì in batches until golden, then drain on kitchen paper. Serve hot to ensure a nice gooey cheese centre.

Gnudi Butter Sauce

INGREDIENTS

GNUDI
250g of ricotta, drained in a sieve lined
with muslin cloth overnight
125g of Pecorino Romano, finely grated
1 small egg
6 tbsp of breadcrumbs
1/4 tsp grated nutmeg
semolina flour
salt

SAGE AND BROWN BUTTER SAUCE
40g of butter
1 handful of sage, leaves picked
1/4 lemon

salt

Method

STEP 1
To make the gnudi, mix together all of
the ingredients, except the semolina, in
a mixing bowl using a wooden spoon

STEP 2
Once fully incorporated, roll the
mixture into neat 2cm balls

STEP 3
Place in a tray dusted with semolina
flour and place in the fridge uncovered
overnight to dry out a little more
image

STEP 4
Cook in salted boiling water until they
rise to the top, then drain and leave to
steam for a minute or so

STEP 5
Meanwhile, place the butter in a large
frying pan on a medium heat. As it
melts, add the sage leaves and add a
sprinkle of salt

STEP 6
Once the butter has completely melted, add the gnudi and turn up the heat a little. Give the pan a shake every now and then to get an even colouring. You need to work quite quickly or the gnudi will become soft and may start to split

STEP 7
Once nice and golden, the butter should have caramelised into a nutty brown butter and the sage will have crisped up

STEP 8
Finish with a squeeze of lemon juice and serve warm.

Gnocchi alla Romana

INGREDIENTS

500ml of milk
30g of butter
salt, to taste
nutmeg, to taste
125g of semolina flour
1 egg yolk
40g of Parmesan, finely grated (plus extra to grate on top before serving)

Method

STEP 1

To begin, bring the milk to a simmer
with a pinch of salt and nutmeg and
whisk in the semolina flour. Stir on a
medium-low heat until the mixture
starts to thicken and pull away from the
sides of the pan. This should take
around 10 minutes

STEP 2

Remove from the heat and stir in the
butter, cheese and egg yolk – make sure
the mixture isn't piping hot as you don't
want to scramble the yolks

STEP 3

Spread the mixture across a
greaseproof-lined tray into a 1.5cm
thick layer and allow to cool

STEP 4

Preheat the oven to 180°C/gas mark 4

STEP 5

Cut the dough into discs using a 4cm
round cutter, then layer neatly into an
ovenproof dish

STEP 6
Grate more Parmesan over the dish and bake for around 25 minutes, or until golden and crispy

STEP 7
Serve up as a vegetarian main with salad, or as a side dish.

Spaghetti Aglio Olio e Peperoncino

INGREDIENTS

450g of spaghetti
60ml of olive oil
6 garlic cloves, peeled and finely chopped
1 red chilli, chopped
4 anchovy fillets, finely chopped or 1 tsp colatura
salt

Method

STEP 1

Cook the pasta in a large pan of boiling salted water for 5–6 minutes or until al dente

STEP 2

Meanwhile, heat the oil in a large saucepan and fry the garlic and chilli gently, without letting them brown. At this point you could add the anchovies and let them dissolve in the oil, or add the colatura. This sauce doesn't take more than 5 minutes to prepare

STEP3

Lift the cooked pasta from the water, using pasta tongs, and mix directly into the sauce. I wouldn't choose to add cheese here, but you can, only if you really insist.

Spaghetti al Pomodoro

INGREDIENTS

1kg tomatoes, (sweet solanato or ripe
cherry tomatoes work best)
1 onion, roughly chopped
12 basil leaves
400g of spaghetti
Parmesan, or ricotta Salata, finely
grated (optional)
3 tbsp of extra virgin olive oil
salt, to taste

Method

STEP 1

To begin, cut a slit in the tomatoes (vertically) and place them in a pan with the chopped onion and a little salt. Squash them a little with a wooden spoon to get the juices out, then cook uncovered on a medium-low heat for 20–30 minutes

STEP 2

Discard any liquids that have accumulated on top by skimming off with a spoon. Scoop the cooked tomatoes and onions out of the pan and place in a vegetable mill. Process the pulp into a bowl. If you don't own a vegetable mill, blitz the tomatoes and onions in a blender then pass through a fine sieve

STEP 3

Place the tomato sauce back onto the heat and cook it again, uncovered, on a medium-low heat until it thickens

STEP 4

Add the torn basil leaves 5 minutes before it's ready and season with salt

STEP 5
Cook the pasta al dente, following the instructions on the packet. Drain and mix in a serving bowl with the tomato sauce

STEP 6
Serve with a drizzle of extra virgin olive oil and finely grated Parmesan, if preferred.

Bucatini all' Amatriciana

INGREDIENTS

100g of guanciale, or good quality
pancetta, diced into 0.5cm cubes
400g of San Marzano tomatoes, (1 tin)
1/2 onion, diced (optional)
1/2 red chilli, diced (optional)
50ml of white wine
olive oil
400g of bucatini pasta
Pecorino Romano, to grate on top
basil leaves, torn

Method

STEP 1
To begin, slowly heat the diced
guanciale with a tablespoon of olive oil
over a medium-low heat. If using
onions and chilli, add them to the pan
to soften in the rendered fat, cooking
them until soft but without colour

STEP 2
Once the guanciale is lightly golden,
add the white wine and reduce by three
quarters

STEP 3
Add the tin of tomatoes (if using whole
tomatoes, roughly chop them first)

STEP 4
Cook down on a low heat for 10–15
minutes until the sauce has thickened.
Taste and add salt and a pinch of sugar
if necessary

STEP 5
Cook the pasta in a pan of heavily
salted boiling water for 8–10 minutes,
or as per packet instructions

STEP 6

Once the pasta is al dente, drain and add it to the sauce, tossing to make sure the pasta is evenly coated

STEP 7

Serve straight away with plenty of grated Pecorino Romano and some torn basil leaves.

Pasta alla norma

INGREDIENTS

4 servings
400g penne rigate or macaroni
500ml tomato sauce
1-2 aubergines
salted ricotta
extra virgin olive oil
1 clove garlic
basil

Method

STEP 1

Cut the eggplants into slices, then salt them and place them in a colander. Leave them like that for half an hour so the liquid that oozes from the eggplants can drain, thus reducing their bitterness.

STEP 2
Sauté the garlic in extra virgin olive oil, then pour in the tomato sauce, season with salt, and cook for 15 minutes. Turn off the heat and stir in the basil.

STEP 3
Fry the eggplant slices in a lot of oil, then cut them into strips, and add those strips to the tomato sauce.

STEP 4
Cook pasta according to the packaging instructions, drain it, then add it to the sauce.

STEP 5
Divide between individual plates, and sprinkle with grated, salted ricotta before serving.

Cacio e Pepe

INGREDIENTS

4 servings
400g spaghetti
180g Pecorino Romano
8 pinches of roasted and crushed
pepper
salt, as needed

FOR SERVING
roasted and crushed pepper and
Pecorino romano, to sprinkle over the
dish, to taste

Method

STEP 1
Roast the peppercorns in a nonstick pan over medium heat, until they start turning translucent.

STEP 2
Then, place the peppercorns on a paper towel to cool. Once cooled, crush them in a mortar and pestle or with the back of a pan, so you end up with pepper that is fine as a powder but interspersed with larger specks of pepper.

STEP 3
Bring a pot of water to a boil, then salt it and throw in the spaghetti to cook until al dente — ideally, boil the spaghetti in a smaller amount of water so you end up with cooking water that has more starch which will help make a creamier sauce.

STEP 4
Add the Pecorino Romano to an aluminum pan, then add four ladlefuls of the hot cooking water, mixing it as you add.

STEP 5
Once the cheese has melted, add the pepper, and add the pasta (take it out of the water using a carving fork or thongs, so there is still water left on the spaghetti) and mix until the sauce coats the spaghetti.

STEP 6
Serve immediately, on a hot plate, sprinkled with pepper and Pecorino Romano.

Spaghetti alle Vongole

INGREDIENTS

4 servings
350 gr spaghetti
1.5 kg carpet-shell clams, cleaned
2 garlic cloves
1 bunch parsley
6 tbsp extra-virgin olive oil
1 tip of the knife of peperoncino,
optional
salt, to taste

Method

STEP 1
Sauté the clams in two tablespoons of olive oil, together with one peeled and crushed garlic clove, and a small amount of previously washed and chopped parsley. Cover with a lid, and cook over high heat until the clams open, shaking the pan from time to time.

STEP 2
Pluck the meat out of the clams, setting aside some of the clam shells for later, while discarding the rest. Filter the cooking liquid. Sauté the remaining garlic clove in four tablespoons of olive oil. Add the peperoncino (optional), clam meat, and the cooking liquid, and sauté for a few minutes.

STEP 3
Next, cook the spaghetti al dente, drain, and put them in the pan with clams, then mix everything well while still on the stove.

STEP 4
Plate and decorate with clam shells and parsley.

Pasta 4 Formaggi

INGREDIENTS

1 Cup macaroni(pasta)
12 cherry tomatoes
1/2 cup milk
1 sprig rosemary
1 sprig thyme
1 Spring onion
2 Garlic cloves
10 gms onions, chopped
10 gms leeks, chopped
10 gms celery, chopped
1 Bay leaf
60 gms butter

30 gms flour
A pinch of white pepper
1/2 tsp nutmeg, grated
15 gms parmesan cheese
20 gms cheddar cheese
15 gms brie cheese
20 gms Swiss emmental cheese
A pinch of chilli flakes

Method

STEP 1
Boil the macaroni in salted water.

STEP 2
After boiling, strain and put in a bowl with olive oil.

STEP 3
Melt the butter with flour in a saucepan along with olive oil.

STEP 4
Boil some milk with rosemary, thyme, bay leaf and spring onions.

STEP 5
Strain the milk in with the flour and butter, whisking slowly.

STEP 6
Make sure you keep stirring the sauce.

STEP 7
Season with salt and pepper.

STEP 8
Once the sauce coats the back of your spoon means it's done.

STEP 9
Grate parmesan, add cheddar, some chunks of brie and emmental.

STEP 10
Put in the sauce and mix it in.

STEP 11
In a hot pan add some slice garlic, cherry tomatoes, chilli flakes and a pinch of salt.

STEP 12
Saute well and deglaze with a touch of white wine.

STEP 13

Mix the macaroni with the sauce and serve.

Pasta al Forno

INGREDIENTS

200 Gram Any short pasta
2 tbsp Olive oil
1 medium Onion, chopped
1 tbsp Garlic (minced)
1 cup Mixed bell peppers
1 cup Mushrooms, sliced
1 cup Spinach (chopped), blanched
1 medium Eggplant
1/2 cup Mixed olives
1-2 Green chillies, chopped
1 cup Tomato puree
2 cups Mixed cheese, grated
1 cup Cream

1/2 cup Breadcrumbs
150 gram Butter (cut into cubes)

Method

STEP 1
Cook the pasta in boiling salted water
for about 9 to 11 minutes.

STEP 2
Drain and lay on to a tray/plate.
STEP 3
In a heavy bottomed pan, heat up some
olive oil.

STEP 4
Add the onions, garlic, chillies and
saute them for 2 minutes.

STEP 5
Add the bell peppers and eggplant and
saute for 2 minutes followed by the
mushrooms, olives and the spinach.

STEP 6
Let this cook for 5 minutes. Then pour
in the tomato puree and the cream.

STEP 7
Season to taste. Take the pan off the stove and mix in the pasta.

STEP 8
Then mix in half the cheese. Pour the mixture into a greased baking dish.

STEP 9
Sprinkle the rest of the cheese evenly topped with the breadcrumbs. Add the cubes of butter over and let it bake in the oven for 20 minutes at 160-180 degrees.

Pasta ai Funghi

INGREDIENTS

50 Gram shitake mushroom (soaked in warm water for 15 minutes)
100 gram fresh mushroom-sliced
1 tbsp onion, chopped
1 garlic clove
1 tbsp fresh thyme or fresh parsley, chopped
30 ml white Wine
100 gram whole wheat pasta-penne or linguine
For seasoning salt and pepper

Method

STEP 1
Put the pasta in boiling salted water for
the time specified on the packet. Whilst
the pasta is boiling prepare the sauce.

STEP 2
In a heavy bottomed saucepan, saute
onion and garlic in olive oil, add
mushroom and wine.

STEP 3
Once the wine has evaporated, add
some of the water in which shitake
mushroom was soaked.

STEP 4
Add salt, herbs and cook for 5-6
minutes.

STEP 5
Once the pasta is cooked, add to the
sauce with a little bit of pasta water.
Serve at once.

Penne alla Vodka

INGREDIENTS

1 Tbsp Butter
1 tbsp Olive oil
1 small Onion, finely chopped
1 tbsp Garlic , chopped
3/4 cup Fresh cream
1/4 cup Vodka
1/4 tsp Chilli flakes
1 can of Italian plum tomatoes
deseeded and chopped (you can use
regular tomatoes also)
2 tbsp Parmesan cheese, grated

Method

STEP 1
Melt butter and olive oil in a saucepan with onion and garlic till translucent.

STEP 2
Add tomatoes and cook till almost no liquid remains in the pan (med-low heat) stirring frequently.

STEP 3
Add cream, vodka and chilli flakes and boil until thickened to sauce consistency.

STEP 4
Season with salt and pepper. Sauce can be made a day ahead and refrigerated.

STEP 5
Cook penne pasta in a large pot of boiling water with salt till al dente.

STEP 6
Transfer to a bowl.bring sauce to simmer and toss pasta. Sprinkle with Parmesan.

Pasta e Patate

INGREDIENTS

1 tbsp extra virgin olive oil
1/4 white onion, finely sliced
2 medium potatoes, peeled and diced
1 tbsp of tomato puree
600 ml (2 1/2 cups) of boiling salted
water

100 g (3 1/2 oz) short pasta
50 g (1 3/4 oz) of crust of Parmesan
cheese, cubed
Red hot chilli pepper or freshly ground
black pepper and grated Parmesan
cheese to serve

Method

STEP 1
Pour the extra virgin olive oil in a
medium sized pot and add the finely
sliced onion. Cook the onion over low
heat for a few minutes, stirring often,
until golden.

STEP 2
Add the diced potatoes and a spoon of
tomato sauce, which will give a pinkish
and inviting colour to the pasta and
potatoes. Stir to mix all the flavour,
then cover with hot salted water.

STEP 3
Cook over low heat for about 10
minutes, then add the short pasta and
the crust of Parmesan cheese and cook
for 10 up to 15 minutes, until the pasta
is cooked. Stir often once you add the

Parmesan crust because the cheese will tend to stick to the bottom of the pan.

STEP 4

When the pasta and the potatoes are cooked through and the cooking liquid has been almost completely absorbed, leaving a thick and creamy soup, remove the pot from the heat and serve with grated Parmigiano Reggiano cheese and a pinch of black pepper or dried chili.

Tortellini in Brodo

INGREDIENTS

BROTH

600g of chicken bones, a carcass or
wings will work too
3l water
1 onion, peeled and halved
1 carrot, peeled
1 stick of celery
1 potato, peeled
salt

PASTA

200g of plain flour, sifted
2 eggs

FILLING
200g of pork loin, finely diced
2 tbsp of unsalted butter
200g of prosciutto, thinly sliced
200g of mortadella, thinly sliced
100g of Parmesan, grated
2 eggs
nutmeg, freshly grated
salt
freshly ground black pepper

TO SERVE
Parmesan, grated

Method

STEP 1
Begin by making the broth. In a large
pot set over a medium heat, combine all
the ingredients for the broth. Bring to a
gentle simmer and cook for 2 hours,
removing any foam that forms on the
surface. Allow the broth to cool slightly,
then remove the chicken bones and
vegetables and pass through a sieve.
Reserve to one side

STEP 2

Whilst the stock is simmering, make the pasta dough. On a work surface, form the flour into a well. Crack the eggs into the centre of the well. Whisk the eggs with a fork, incorporating the flour a little at a time, until the dough starts to come together. Carry on with your hands, kneading the dough until you have a smooth, elastic ball. Flatten into a disc, wrap in cling film and leave to rest for 30 minutes in the fridge

STEP 3

While the pasta is resting, make the filling. Melt the butter in a frying pan set over a medium heat. Brown the pork on all sides. Remove from the heat and use a knife to mince it together with the prosciutto and mortadella. Combine the meat with the Parmesan and eggs, then season to taste with salt, pepper and nutmeg

STEP 4

Divide the pasta dough into 3 pieces. Roll the balls out on a pasta machine, starting on the widest setting and moving progressively down to the lowest. Spread the sheets over a floured work surface. Cut each sheet into 3cm squares, then place a small amount of the filling onto each square (about half a teaspoon). Fold the square diagonally in half onto itself to form a triangle, then fold it again so that the corners at the bases come together to form a pocket. Whilst you are forming the pasta try to squeeze out any air bubbles, as these will expand and burst. Use a little water to seal the pasta together if needed

STEP 5
Once you have sealed all the tortellini, reheat the broth. Season to taste and, once simmering, add the tortellini. Cook for about a minute, then remove from the heat

STEP 6
Divide the tortellini and broth between 6 serving bowls and top with grated Parmesan.

Pasta e Zucchine

INGREDIENTS

Kosher salt, to taste
1 lb. mezzi rigatoni or other short pasta
1 lb. green beans, cut into 1 1/2-inch
pieces
1 medium zucchini
1/4 c. sliced almonds
2 garlic cloves
1 c. fresh parsley
1/2 c. fresh tarragon

1/3 c. plus 2 tablespoons olive oil
1/2 c. grated parmesan cheese, plus
more for topping
Black pepper, to taste
1 lb. yellow summer squash, cut into
half-moons
3/4 c. heavy cream

Method

STEP 1
Bring a large pot of salted water to a
boil. Add the pasta and cook according
to the package directions, adding the
green beans during the last 2 minutes.
Reserve 1 cup cooking water, then drain
the pasta and green beans and place in
a large bowl.

STEP 2
Meanwhile, slice the zucchini in half
lengthwise. Use a spoon to scrape out
the seeds. Chop the zucchini into
½-inch pieces.

STEP 3
Make the pesto: Place the almonds and
garlic in a food processor and pulse
until finely chopped. Add the parsley,

tarragon and zucchini and pulse until finely chopped. With the machine running, slowly drizzle in 1/3 cup olive oil and process until fairly smooth. Scrape into a bowl and mix in the parmesan and season with salt and pepper.

STEP 4
Heat the remaining 2 tablespoons olive oil in a large skillet over medium-high heat. Add the yellow squash, season with salt and pepper and cook, stirring, until browned, 4 to 5 minutes.

STEP 5
Add the heavy cream to the skillet and stir. Reduce the heat to low and let thicken slightly, about 2 minutes. Mix in the pesto until evenly distributed.

STEP 6
the pesto mixture to the pasta and green beans and toss, adding the reserved cooking water as needed to loosen. Serve with more parmesan for topping.

Pasta Carciofi e Spinaci

INGREDIENTS

6 tbsp. Butter
4 cloves Garlic, Finely Minced
2 bags Baby Spinach
2 cans Artichoke Hearts, Drained And Halved
3 tbsp. Flour
3 c. Whole Milk
1/4 tsp. Cayenne Pepper
Salt And Pepper, to taste
1/2 c. Grated Parmesan Cheese

1 1/2 c. Mozzarella Or Monterey Jack Cheese, Grated
1/2 c. Low Sodium Chicken Broth (less Or More)
12 oz. weight Penne, Cooked Until Al Dente
1/2 c. Seasoned Panko Breadcrumbs
Crushed Red Pepper, To Taste

Method

STEP 1
Melt 2 tablespoons butter in a large pot or skillet. Add garlic and throw in the spinach. Stir it around until it's wilted, about 1 minute. Remove spinach from heat and set aside.

STEP 2
Add 2 tablespoons butter to the same pot and raise the heat to high. Throw in the halved artichokes and stir it around until they get a little color, 1 to 2 minutes. Remove the artichokes from the pot and set them aside.

STEP 3
Reduce the heat to low. Add 2 tablespoons butter to the pot. When

melted, sprinkle in flour and whisk until it's combined. Pour in milk and whisk to combine. Let it cook for 3 to 4 minutes, or until starting to thicken. Add Parmesan, Mozzarella/Monterey Jack, salt and pepper, and cayenne pepper. Stir to melt, and if it's overly thick, splash in chicken broth.

STEP 4

Add artichokes and pasta, tossing gently to combine. Gently fold in spinach, then pour the pasta into a serving bowl. Sprinkle the top with crushed red pepper flakes and plenty of Panko breadcrumbs for crunch.

Frittata di Spaghetti

INGREDIENTS

4-5 eggs
A very generous handful of freshly
grated Parmigiano Reggiano PDO
Salt and pepper to taste
1 portion of leftover Pasta al Pomodoro
(about 80 grams of dried pasta, cooked
and tossed in a tomato sauce)
Italian extra virgin olive oil
Fresh herbs such as parsley, basil or
oregano

Method

STEP 1
Beat together the eggs and cheese until
creamy. Season with salt and plenty of
cracked pepper.

STEP 2
Oil an ovenproof frying pan generously
with Italian extra virgin olive oil and
place over a low flame.

STEP 3
Arrange your spaghetti over the entire
pan to cover it evenly.

STEP 4
Allow to cook for 1 minute before
pouring over the eggs – try to cover the
pan evenly.

Rigatoni alla Genovese

INGREDIENTS

1 tablespoon olive oil
6 ounces pancetta or salt pork, diced
2 ½ pounds beef chuck
2 teaspoons kosher salt
½ cup diced celery
½ cup diced carrot
1 teaspoon kosher salt
1 teaspoon freshly ground black pepper
1 tablespoon tomato paste
1 bay leaf
⅔ cup white wine

4 pounds yellow onions, sliced
2 pounds red onions, sliced
salt to taste
2 (16 ounce) boxes uncooked rigatoni
1 tablespoon chopped fresh marjoram
leaves
1 pinch cayenne pepper
2 tablespoons freshly grated
Parmigiano-Reggiano cheese

Method

STEP 1
Heat oil in a large pot over medium
heat. Cook pancetta until most of the
fat is rendered out, about 6 minutes.
Remove cooked pancetta with a slotted
spoon and save.

STEP 2
Raise heat to high and transfer meat to
the pot. Season with salt. Cook and stir
until liquid releases from beef and
begins to evaporate, and meat browns,
10 to 15 minutes.

STEP 3
Reduce heat to medium-high. Add
celery, carrots, reserved cooked

pancetta, salt and pepper. Cook and stir for about 5 minutes. Add a heaping tablespoon of tomato paste, bay leaf, and white wine. Cook and stir, scraping up the brownings from the bottom of the pan, 2 to 3 minutes. Add sliced onions. Reduce heat to medium. Cover pot and cook for 30 minutes without stirring. After 30 minutes, stir onions and meat until well mixed. Cover again, and cook for another 30 minutes. Stir.

STEP 4
Reduce heat to low and cook uncovered 8 to 10 hours, stirring occasionally. Skim off fat as mixture cooks. If sauce seems to reduce too much, add water or broth as needed to maintain a sauce-like consistency. Cook until beef and onions seem to melt into each other.

STEP 5
Bring a large pot of lightly salted water to a boil. Cook rigatoni in the boiling water, stirring occasionally until just barely al dente, 10 to 12 minutes. Drain.

STEP 6

Add rigatoni to the sauce and cook until heated through. Serve topped with a pinch of marjoram and freshly grated Parmigiano-Reggiano cheese.

Pasta e Ceci

INGREDIENTS

1 tablespoon olive oil
1 medium onion, diced
1 medium carrot, diced
1 medium celery stalk, diced
4 garlic cloves, minced
4 cup vegetable broth
1 (14 ounce or 400 gram) can diced
tomatoes
1 (14 ounce or 400 gram) can
chickpeas, drained and rinsed

1 tablespoon finely chopped fresh
rosemary
1 cup dried ditalini pasta (or another
type of small pasta)
Salt and pepper, to tastes

Method

STEP 1
Coat the bottom of a large pot with
olive oil and place it over medium heat.

STEP 2
Give the oil a minute to heat up, and
then add the onion, carrot, and celery.
Sweat the veggies for about 10 minutes,
until they begin to soften up.

STEP 3
Add the garlic and cook for about 1
minute more, until very fragrant.

STEP 4
Stir in the broth, tomatoes, chickpeas,
and rosemary.

STEP 5

Bring the liquid to a boil, reduce the heat, and allow it to simmer for about 10 minutes.

STEP 6
Stir in the pasta and bring the liquid back up to a boil.

STEP 7
Allow the pasta to cook in the soup at a low boil until al dente — this may take a minute or two longer than the time indicated on the pasta's package directions. Stir the pot occasionally while it simmers.

STEP 8
Remove the pot from the heat and season with salt and pepper to taste.

STEP 9
Ladle into bowls and serve.

Orecchiette alle Cime di Rapa

INGREDIENTS

250g of orecchiette, fresh
3 garlic cloves, sliced
1/2 red chilli, sliced
5 anchovies
200g of broccoli rabe, or tenderstem broccoli
pecorino, to serve (optional)

Method

STEP 1
Begin by making and cooking the orecchiette (you can use shop-bought, if preferred) and cooking it in salted boiling water

STEP 2
Meanwhile, gently fry the garlic and chilli with the anchovies in a little of their oil until the has softened a little and the anchovies have dissolved

STEP 3
2 minutes before the pasta is ready, add the broccoli rabe to the pasta pan to cook

STEP 4
Drain, then add the pasta and broccoli to the anchovy pan and toss to coat the pasta evenly

STEP 5
Serve hot with an extra drizzle of olive oil, plus a little grated pecorino, if desired.

Pasta e Salmone

INGREDIENTS

500g (1 lb) fettuccine or other pasta
250g (8 oz) smoked salmon, roughly
cut up
500ml (1 pint) heavy (aka double)
cream
Salt and pepper

Method

STEP 1
Cook your pasta al dente in well-salted
boiling water.

STEP 2

Meanwhile, melt some butter in a skillet, then add heavy cream and roughly cut up smoked salmon. Simmer until the cream has reduced to a saucy consistency and the salmon has imparted it's wonderful flavor to the cream.

STEP 3

Add your cooked fettuccine to the sauce and toss. Add a bit more cream if need be, making sure that the pasta still 'flows' rather loosely—fresh pasta tends to absorb its sauce quickly, and creamy ones especially quickly.

STEP 4

Serve your Smoked Salmon Fettuccine right away. No pasta should wait, but this one especially.

Pasta Prosciutto e Piselli

INGREDIENTS

15 oz penne pasta
2/3 cup prosciutto - ham (cubed)
2/3 cup piselli - green peas (fresh or frozen)
3/4 cup panna - half and half or cream
3 TBS butter
1 TBS flour
1/4 tsp nutmeg
2 to 3 TBS salt (to taste)

Method

STEP 1
Cube ham into small 1/4 inch pieces
In a large pot, add 6 quarts of water,
bring to boil - add salt to taste like the
sea

STEP 2
Lower temperature on the water to
medium high, add penne pasta, return
to boil, and cook according to package
directions until al dente

STEP 3
While pasta is cooking, melt butter in a
large saucepan
Saute ham in the saucepan to warm
Add cream to saucepan, with a 1/4 cup
reserved
Whisk in 1 TBS flour into the 1/4 cup
reserved cream, stir into ham and
cream, until thickened

STEP 4
While ham is sauteing, place green peas
into a strainer and run under warm
water to thaw if frozen, drain peas well
Add peas to ham and cream

Drain pasta, reserving about 1/2 to 1 cup of pasta water

STEP 5
Stir pasta into ham, sauce, and peas; add a little bit of pasta water at a time if sauce is too thick. Continue to add until consistency is right for you.

STEP 6
Taste for salt, add more as needed
Sprinkle with a dash of nutmeg
Serve warm with grated parmesan cheese on the side.